YoungWriters

Dedicated to
You

Young Writers

First published in Great Britain in 2006 by:
Young Writers
Remus House
Coltsfoot Drive
Peterborough
PE2 9JX
Telephone: 01733 890066
Website: www.youngwriters.co.uk
All Rights Reserved
© Copyright Contributors 2006
SB ISBN 1-84602-709-8

Foreword

From all the entries we receive year in year out at Young Writers, it's clear to us that many children love writing about the important people in their lives. We thought what nicer way to celebrate those special people in our lives than to invite our younger generation to dedicate a poem to them to show, with love and respect, what makes that special person truly inspiring.

We are therefore proud to present 'Dedicated To You', a collection of moving poetry written by 7-18 year-olds. So much thought and effort has been put into each poem and we enjoyed reading every single one. This has proved to be a unique opportunity for all involved. Not only does it give the writer a chance to have their work published, but also to let those closest know how much they are appreciated.

Young Writers was established in 1991 to promote poetry and creative writing to school children and encourage them to read, write and enjoy it. Here at Young Writers we are sure you'll agree that this fantastic edition achieves our aim and celebrates today's wealth of young writing talent. We hope you and your family continue to enjoy 'Dedicated To You' for many years to come and hopefully inspire others to put pen to paper

Contents

The Poems

Birthday Message For Dad

Here's a special thing today,
I love you in each and every way,
Just remember, when England play,
You'll be turning 35!
In a couple of years, you'll need this advice,
Some anti-wrinkle cream would be nice,
As you'll soon be getting old,
Your wrinkles will become very bold,
Just remember before you go, Scrudado,
There is a special place in my heart for you.

Olivia Frary (11)

My Best Friend

My best friend makes me happy,
When I am feeling sad,
My best friend makes me feel good,
When I am feeling bad.

My best friend keeps a secret,
She would never break my heart,
My best friend's always with me,
We will never be apart.

My best friend always helps me,
When I don't know what to do
And in return for her kindness,
I try to help her too.

We tell each other our problems
And all our feelings felt,
Then we work them out together
And make undealt problems dealt.

When I am feeling upset,
She will always dry my tears
And when I am feeling frightened,
She will always comfort my fears.

Whenever I'm about to give up
And I am all out of hope,
She would say, in an optimistic voice,
'I will help you cope.'

My best friend would always support me,
In a difficult situation,
My best friend would always call me,
Even if she's across the nation.

My best friend always plays with me,
Even if I'm feeling down,
Then she'll ask me, 'What's wrong?'
And she'll take a smile from a frown.

I thank God very dearly,
For giving me such a friend
And I hope that Emma's and my friendship,
Will never, ever end.

Gabriella Mary Lena Coughlan (10)

My Friend Tom

Tom's a good friend
I've known him for years
He's got blond hair
And sticky-out ears

He's brilliant at games
Especially sport
Although he is small
And quite short

The reason I like him
Well, I'm not sure why
It's just the fact
He's a brilliant guy

He's clever and kind
A really great friend
And on that note
I think I will end!

Megan Wardroper (10)

All Sisters Are Annoying, But My Sister's The Best!

I can't wait to see her, she really is the best,
I feel so excited, I cannot take a rest,
I'm so fond of her, I see her when I blink,
That's only 'cause she's beautiful and she never ever stinks!

She'd do a hit in Bollywood,
She's really, really, really good,
She says that I'm her bestest sister,
She does not say bad lies and twisters,
My love for her would fill the world,
She'd give a kiss heart-shaped and pearled!

Her face always smiles, with all good grace,
She runs to the base and then wins the race,
She gets to the park and plays fun games
And then she learns other people's new names.

I love my sister, I love her to bits,
If I didn't see her, I'd have all the fits!

Nadia Chowdhury (10)

Someone Special

Emily is my friend,
I like her all the time,
Emily is my friend,
We sometimes sing a rhyme.

Emily is my friend,
We both like the fairy books,
Emily is my friend,
We always have the latest looks.

Elizabeth Shearman (8)

My Dad

My dad is like a lion,
Courageous and very proud,
He's also quite understanding,
My dad stands out in a crowd.

My dad is like a donkey,
Working so hard, day after day,
Doing things without complaining,
More than a donkey pulling cart loads of hay.

My dad is like . . .
Amazing really,
So I thank you Dad, for being so special
And having so many good qualities.

Yasmin Burton (11)

My Mum And My Dad

I love my mum and dad
They're loving to me
They always come outside
And play with me

My mum baths me
Tucks me in at night
Reads me a story
Then says, 'Night, night'

When I get up
My breakfast is there
I love my mum
She really cares

My dad takes me
To the park to play
I love my dad
What more can I say?

Mark Bailey (9)

Tigger

Tigger is my mum
She never sits down
Always jumps up now, now, now
Does the tidying
And lots more
When will she stop?
Please now, please now
That is my mum.

Belinda Massmann-Oakley (12)

My Mom

I thank my mom for looking after me,
I thank my mom for all the care and share,
She's better than the rest, that's obvious,
With all the time she puts in for me,
My mom loves me, you see
And that's why I say thank you,
For all her generosity and love for me.

Hayley Garner (11)

Number One!

Mum, through all the sadness and tears,
You have helped me cope all these years,

Young at heart - but wise in thought,
Thanks for teaching me all you have been taught.

I may have said you're horrible, but that is not the truth,
With all your kisses and cuddles, I never have the proof.

Buying me expensive gifts above the budget price,
Although all the little presents are just as nice.

Dogs, ducks, sheep, geese and all the rest,
I have to say, are the best.

But even if we had none of these, I'd be fine,
Due to my mummy's love being close to mine.

I'm thanking you for lots of fun,
'Cause Mother, you're *number one!*

Jay Semmler (12)

My Mum!

My mum, she is the best,
She's better than the rest,
She is very kind
And has a good mind
My mum, she *is* the best!

Fatema Parlin (11)

Mum

The one that does the cooking,
The one who does the chores,
The one who does the dishes,
The one who sweeps the floors.

The one who lays the table,
The one who runs our bath,
The one who gives us cuddles,
The one who makes us laugh.

The one who gives us pocket money,
The mum who does everything,
Surely we could do all that,
For her special day in spring!

Vicky Swain (10)

My Mum

My mum is fantastic and is very, very funny,
When I'm at school and she's at work, she brings me home a bunny.
I love her lots and lots and lots,
She is the most amazing
And I love her more than anyone,
She is the
Best
Best
Best
Mum ever!

Hannah Abigail Powlesland (8)

Super Mum

My mum is great,
She lets me go on my trampoline with my mate.
I sit in the sun and Mum goes out
And brings back a chocolate bun.
I have so much fun, me and my mum!

Emma Jane Phillips (9)

My Mom Is . . .

My mom is great,
My mom is kind,
Give her an errand,
She doesn't mind!

My mom can play,
All day long!
If there's a new hit,
She'll learn the song!

My mom loves pets,
My mom loves me,
My mom loves everyone,
In the family!

My mom can cook,
My mom can clean,
My mom is protective
And never mean!

My mom is great,
My mom is kind,
Give her an errand,
She doesn't mind!

Jade Wilde (12)

My Mom's The Best!

My mom is special to me,
She's always there when I need her,
She keeps things tidy around the house,
My mom's the best!

My mom is special to me,
She's loving and warm,
She cares for me,
My mom's the best!

My mom is special to me,
She's perfect is every way,
She loves us all,
My mom's the best!

My mom is special to me,
She helps me walk the dog,
Her food is delicious,
My mom's the best!

My mom is special to me,
She's always there when I need her,
She keeps things tidy around the house,
My mom's the best!

Sophie Ball (12)

Sisterly

(To my big sister, Maria)

I know we've had our ups and downs,
Where we've both felt very sad,
But even through my selfishness,
You've always held my hand.
I think back to the moments when we argue and we cry,
But it's hard not to forget moments when we laugh,
can't stop even when we try.
You've guided me through everything,
I owe a lot to you,
Your advice, your thoughts, your wishes,
Always show right through.
I know I haven't been that great,
As far as sisters go,
But whenever I've had a problem,
The answer you will always know.
We finish each other's sentences,
A connection quite rare,
One that only sisters,
Us lucky ones can bare.
I know you'll back me up,
In any dreams I have,
Yet you show me all the truth,
Even when it's bad.
You tell it as it is,
You're not afraid to say,
Your beliefs are very strong,
Ones you can't betray.
I ask of you so many things,
Yet you never complain,
My wishful thinking and airy ways,
I know must be hard to live with,
But you do it every day.
You've been there since the day I was born,
In every memory,
I guess sis, what I try to say,
Is that, without you, there never would have been a me,
Like me.

Anna Goodhew (12)

Mom

My mom is special and this is why,
She cleans my room and cooks me pie.
She loves and cares for all of us
And never, ever makes a fuss
About all the things she has to do,
Like cook the tea and buy shampoo.

Mom always has a smile on her face,
When she's finished cleaning,
The house is no disgrace.

She cooks us really nice food for tea,
She cooks for me and my family.

And when I'm tired and it's time for bed,
She tucks me up and I rest my head,
When she tucks me up, she kisses my brow,
Says, 'Goodnight' and 'Time for sleep now.'

Beth Rogerson (12)

My Mum

A happy bird chirping around,
As high as a kite, never coming down,
A steaming train puffing out smoke,
A stressed human with a little hope,
A lovely tulip brightening the day,
A dancing monkey who likes to play,
An ongoing heartbeat never giving up,
A healthy panther says her horoscope,
An amazing swimmer, like a shark,
As ferocious as a lion on a bad day,
A boomerang that will never stay away!

Tamara Williams (12)

My Super Mum

My mum gave life to me,
She was there when I took my first steps,
She was there when I said my first word,
She's there to tuck me in and kiss me goodnight,
What I'm trying to say,
On this really special day, is . . .
I love you, Mum!

Anila Abbas (10)

My Mum

Every day it's the same,
Someone's calling her name,
'Can I have this and that
And maybe just a chat?'

'I'm busy, but come here,
What's the matter, dear?
I'm listening,
For everything.'

'You can play pretend,
I am your friend,
We'll have chips for tea,
You can talk to me.'

'We'll have a party,
We'll be arty,
We'll have some fun,
Till the day is done.'

'Now go to sleep,
Without a peep,
Sleep tight, without fright,
Have a good night.'

Matthew Jaggar (12)

My Mum

A special person to me, is my mum,
She's happy, joyful and she's always there for me,
But when she's mad, she'll blow up like a bomb!

My mum is a mum who cares,
She cares, but does not have the best of luck,
At night-time if I ask,
She'll read me my favourite story.

When I'm really warm,
She turns the heating off at home,
But I can't have a dog,
So I try not to moan!

She's always on the phone,
She never chews a bone,
She's so loving and caring,
So I'm never alone.

Jasmin Smith (12)

My Dad

My dad is cool,
He loves football,
He plays with me
And drinks his tea.
I love my dad,
He is very glad.
He is good at sport
And well taught.
He is very good at pool
And he also rules.
My dad hates cats
And also rats.
My dad loves me
And I am happy.

Benjamin Thomas (9)

My Uncle Gal And Auntie Aimee

My Uncle Gal and Auntie Aimee,
Are really very, very crazy,
Even now they always tease me,
They would always give up with ease.

My Uncle Gal and Auntie Aimee,
Are both footie crazy,
They are both super fun,
I love them more than a tonne.

Elizabeth Emery (11)

My Dad

My dad is very weird
My dad is very funny
My dad says he's too old
My dad hops like a bunny

My dad makes me jump high
When I'm on my trampoline
When I'm bouncing
I think I'm gonna scream

When we watch Dr Who
We get so excited
When it is finished
We are delighted.

Roselind Hinwood (9)

Double M

Everyone is different,
But they all make us smile,
Famous or furry, friend or family,
But my mum's unforgettable.
Her smile makes me feel special
And her cuddles are warm,
So, I know I don't tell her enough,
But Mum, I will love you all my life.

Sadie Bridger (11)

To My Mum

You seem to be busy in this modern world,
We don't get time to express our feelings to one another,
So listen to what I have to say,
I'm happy and proud to have a mum like you
And will always love you.

Fatimah Zohra (15)

My Mom Is . . .

I love my mom so much,
She is the best
She's loving, caring and kind.

She is pretty
And has got lovely hair,
I love her so much!

She cooks, cleans and tidies up
After my dad,
I love my mom!

My mom's fun, hard-working and so much more
And that's my mom,
I love her!

Rylie Jones (12)

My Dad

My dad is *fantastic!*
He understands me all the time
And is always there for me, no matter what.
He is the best dad in the world and I love him dearly,
I love his fresh, minty breath and strong-smelling deodorant.
My dad has a perfectly nice taste in clothes,
Well, that is what I think.
He wears suits to work and at the weekend he wears a woolly jumper
And jeans or a short-sleeved top and shorts.
I sometimes call him Dad,
But I love to call him Daddy.

Rebecca Page (11)

He Who Must Be Obeyed

He likes a laugh and a joke
He is quite a funny bloke

Pull my finger, what a smell
He asks me how to spell

He is there to scream and shout
He is there to help me out

He is there when I am sad
He is called . . . my dad!

Callum Hudson (9)

My Mum

My mum is so helpful,
She is so joyful,
My mum will help me along my way,
No matter what I say.

Her hair's just like mine,
But I'm only nine,
She will help my writing,
But she's no good at fixing lighting.

All I'm trying to tell you
Is my mum is the best,
She never has time for a rest,
With us three running around,
This poem is coming to an end,
So I'll just put it on the ground . . .

Abbie Murphy (9)

About A Flower Mum

The flower is a beautiful orange,
Pretty and very colourful,
As pretty as my mum.
It makes her feel happy
Like a red-hot summer's day,
That's how nice my mum can be.

Alisha Crook (9)

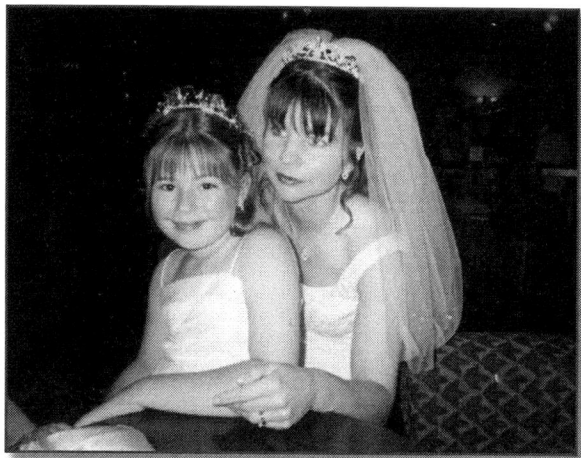

My Mother!

M y mum is kind although sometimes she gets angry
O thers admire her too, meaning my family
T imes at which she plays with me and my sister
H appy times all of the family has
E very week we all play together, but some we may not
R eally, really kind is she, buying things for me and my sister.

Munisha Boora (11)

My Special Mum

My mother is my alarm so bold,
A chirpy bird who sings on the oak,
Outside my window it rains so cold,
But, not with drops do I get soaked.

But with peace and kindness pouring down,
I get caught up in a storm of love,
A smile prevails and I do not frown,
My mum, an angel sent from above.

Summer, winter, spring or fall,
Twenty-four hours of every day,
My mother is fair, not ever cruel,
She takes care of me in every way.

What would I do if my mum wasn't there?
I would throw my hands up in despair,
A puzzle not solved, my life starts to tear,
My mother is there,
        Without a care,
                But to always be there,
                        Must show a deep care.

Vicky Wilton (13)

My Mum

She cooks me tea
And she buys me toys
Yes, she really does love me
She gives me sweets
And she is the best
Yes, I get lots of treats!

Hannah Swann (12)

My Mother

When I look into my future
I hope and pray that I can be
As lovely a mother to my kids
As you are to me

Sometimes I sit and watch you work
But I never see you glum
Always doing your best for us
I really love you Mum

And as I travel life's winding road
And suffer its highs and lows
I'll look back for my inspiration
As only a mother knows

And as I watch my children grow
Through laughter, pain and tears
I'll thank you Mom for all the love
You've given me through the years.

Kirsty Willetts

Happy Mother's Day!

My mom is someone special
There is no one else like her
She is the one who cares for me
She always has time for me.

Even though she is always chatting on the phone
She would never leave me on my own.

Super, terrific, special Mom
You're a superhero
Doing all the household chores
Although you're always making up stupid household laws.

She's always on a diet and having fun
Uh oh, she just ate a hot cross bun!

This is a message to my mom
On this special day
So I sent it off to you on a Friday
In hope that it will come to you on . . .

Happy Mother's Day!

Sarah Nock (13)

Mom

I love you to bits, Mom,
You're the greatest,
In the whole world.

You are the one that's there for me if I've had a bad day
You're the one that supports me in a test
You're the one that will always be best
You're the one that makes all the plans
You're the one that helps me if I'm lost
You're the one to fix something even at a cost.

You're the one that I feel proud of in front of all my mates
You're the one to help me with my cooking
You're the one to help with homework
You're the one that picks the best clothes
You're the one that always knows
You're the one with great fashion.

You're the one to clean and cook
You're the one that helped me read my first book
You're the one that settles quarrels
You're the one that nags about my blinds
You're the one that always reminds . . .

Just how much I love you!

Mai Harrison (12)

For My Mom

Well, where do you start with such a great mom?

Love is a precious treasure
Which she gives to me each day
She's always busy with the things
That need to be done for me

When I'm sad, she makes me happy
When I'm ill, she looks after me
When I need help, she offers it to me
When it's teatime, she makes it for me
When my clothes need washing and ironing, she does that for me
When I do something good, she gives me praise
When I feel down, she'll help me all she can
When we need her, she's there for my brother, my dad and me.

Nicholas Holmes (12)

My Mum

Who is there to clean the house?
Who is there to get rid of the mouse?
Who is there for us when we fall?
Who was there when we were small?
Our mum of course!
We would be lost without her,
We would not change her for a thing,
She is more precious than a diamond ring!

Kelly Sambucci (9)

My Mum

My mum is a strong table
She's a cuddly rabbit
A warm, sunny beach
Birdsong in the morning
She's a peaceful summer afternoon
I love my mum.

Susan Cooperwhite (10)

My Mum

My mum's kind
My mum's sweet
She may be stubborn
She may be mean
But she loves me all the same!

Megan Hails (11)

Thank You Mum

Thank you Mum,
You're always there,
To pick me up from school
And to chant the Lord's Prayer.

I admire you Mum,
How you're always carrying on,
Never giving up,
You never even stop to yawn.

Even Dad admires you,
How clever that you seem to be,
You're so much different from other mums,
You even have a beautiful admiration in birch trees.

Thank you Mum,
You're always there,
To pick me up from school
And to chant the Lord's Prayer.

Harjun Punni (11)

Sadie-Raya

Sadie-Raya is my sister,
Last March, she turned just two,
My family didn't seem to need my help,
I didn't know what I could do!

I remember last winter,
When outside was drenched in rain,
I danced and sang for hours,
To keep dear Sadie entertained!

And at my granny's birthday,
When boredom was at its tip,
Like a volcano erupting -
Sadie let it rip!

One tiresome school day morning,
I refused to get up for air
And my dad let her loose,
On my bed to pull my hair!

Sadie-Raya is my sister,
Last March she turned just two,
My family may not need my help,
But Sadie, that's not true!

Hana Berggren (12)

People Who Are Special To Me

Special Lucy
Lucy is very special to me
She sometimes comes for tea
I'm the lock and she's the key
We will always be together, yes her and me.

Special Hannah
Hannah is great
She's my mate
On my birthday, she's never late
We like to create.

Special Holly
My mate is Holly
She's always jolly
She's got a nice dolly
Her name is Polly.

Lydia Derbyshire (10)

Dads Are Special

D ad, you're the best
A nd can cope anywhere
D ad, you're just amazing
S ometimes sad . . .

A re you OK?
R eply, may you, please
E verywhere, I'll be with you

S pecial you are
P lease never change
E ven if you may move away
C an you please still love me
I n any condition
A nd I will always be by your side
L oving you still.

Lucy McLoughlin (9)

My Auntie Brenda

Brenda you are the best
You really do stand out from the rest

Other times when I am sad
You lift me up and make me glad

Brenda your smile really does run a mile

When I am sad or upset
You lift me up and make me my best

Brenda I just want you to know
You're the best auntie ever!

Gillian Carson (10)

My Special Daddy

My dad is always there for me
Even if he's busy making tea
We go to concerts and other places
But only if there are any spaces

My dad loves football
And he's always on the ball
He supports Luton
But he also supports England

He goes to all the home games
But never gets the blame
He is a cool Dad
And he never goes mad
He loves me so much
That he's never in a rush

My dad is so kind
He never leaves me behind
So all in all
He is so tall
But does it matter?
No, no, not at all!

Roxanne Bacon (12)

Birthday Bumps

Hey, little Matty, you've turned ten
I'll have to give you once again
Something you hate and you'll never love
Only given to you off your big bruv
Have a guess what it is
No, it isn't a great big kiss
It won't hurt that much you'll cry
But you will think I'm an evil guy
It will hurt for the whole of the day
Birthday bumps, that's all I'll say!

Tom Sewell (13)

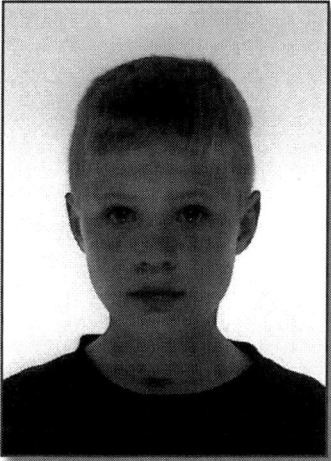

My Dad

My dad is sporty
And he thinks I'm naughty,
My dad is funny,
He loves it when it's sunny.

My dad thinks I'm great
And I'm his best mate,
My dad has always got a smile on his face,
He taught me how to tie my lace.

My dad is fun,
He likes it when he's won,
That's my dad!

Tom Rowlands (12)

My Sister

My sister has a lovely smile,
It always seems to stay on for a while,
Her hair is brown and faintly curly,
Her teeth are white and very pearly,
She is kind and very sweet
And she is a lovely person to meet,
An 'A' is her normal grade,
Her cleverness will never fade,
Her favourite season is the summer,
With her around, it is always funnier,
That is why I love her,
My sister.

Stella Tselingas (12)

A Poem For Mum

How much I love you, I can't say
It's more than words can hold
You are my mother and my friend
My potter and my mould

Yours are the words that shaped my voice
Yours is the spirit within mine
Yours is the will that shaped my choice
You are my fortune and my sign

Our friendship and love shall never end
To me, you are so special
You are my mother and my friend
My guardian angel

When I turn, you're there for me
When I speak, you understand
I feel cared for, but also free
You lead but don't command

I'm fortunate that I was born
To someone just like you
I love you, not just as my mum
But for what you are and do.

Liana Akimova (14)

My Mum

Bouquets and chocolates can never show,
How much I love you, I love you so,
You keep me safe, fed and warm,
Don't wake me up at the crack of dawn!

I do love you so, 'cause you're my mum,
You make me happy when I am glum,
So basically, what I'm trying to say,
Is I will love you till my dying day!

Eleanor Marlow (10)

Poem For My Mum

My mum is special,
Always caring for me,
Helping me around the house,
She gives me kisses and cuddles,
She loves me and I love her too.

Alice Cropper (9)

I Love My Mum

My mum's very special,
She's also very kind,
She's always very caring
And she loves me all the time.
We're always very happy
And having fun together,
She always listens to me
And nurses me when I'm sick.
She also helps me with my homework
And cheers me up when I'm feeling down,
We do lots of things together,
I'll love my mum forever.

Simran Basi (12)

Poem For My Dad

My dad is so kind to me
He picks me up when I am down
He is always there for me.

My dad is so funny
I am left in stitches on the floor
He is so caring.

My dad is the best dad in the world
He is always there when you need him most
My dad is the best dad in the whole world
I couldn't wish for a better dad.

Thank you Dad.

Kelly Foster (12)

Dad

Dad you are the best,
You always make me laugh,
Dad you are so special,
Dad you're number one,
Dad you are so cool,
But you really don't rule,
Dad you're such fun,
Dad you love to run,
Dad you are better than any other dad.

Lauren Tancock (12)

A Friend

A friend can send you round the bend,
But they'll always be your friend.
We have been friends since we were eight
And we'll always be best mates.
When she was on vacation, I missed her,
She's always been like a sister.

Emma Buttery (11)

My Mum

My mum is the best I hope you can tell
She gave me a crib and a life as well
She raised me up and stuck by my side
We've had our arguments, let's put them aside
I know I'm a pain, a nuisance and a bother
But I just want to say, you're the perfect mother!

Luke Jones (12)

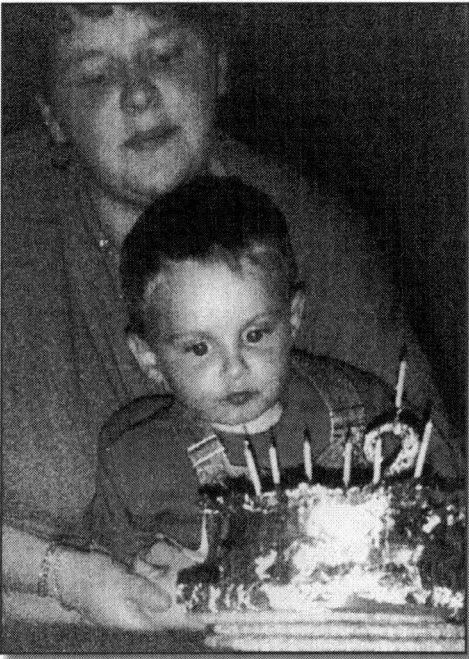

My Mum

Mummy,
Mummy,
I started off
In your tummy.

You've cooked,
You've cleaned,
You're the best mum ever
And exactly what I dreamed.

You're a breath of inspiration,
That's all I can say,
You're the best mum in the world
And that's the same every day.

Alex Elizabeth Drake (11)

My Mum

My mum is the best
My mum will never let me go
My mum is the best
I'll never stop loving her, never, ever
My mum is the best
Mum, I love you so much
My mum is the best
I never want to leave you, ever!

Jasmine Copland (8)

Mother's Day Poem!

My mum is a very good cook,
She's as gorgeous as she looks.
My mum is a busy-body,
But she never used to like Noddy.
When we're playing out,
She loves to dance about.
Her favourite colours are black and white
And she is very scared of heights.
She loves to watch her drama
And her favourite animal is a llama.
At thirty-six years old,
She really feels the cold.
But she's still my mum
And whenever I do something good
She raises her thumb.
But I'm still not too old
For a smack on my bum!

Alleyah Ali (9)

A Poem About My Mum

My mum is fit for a sport,
Even though she is really short,
She is important to me,
One day, she could be a celebrity.

She is quick and fast,
She never comes last,
She is always on the move,
She can really feel the groove.

I love my mum,
If I'm naughty, I bite my thumb,
My mum is strong,
But all she hears is a *ding-dong!*

Umar Ali (8)

My Mum

My mum likes roses, tulips and all sorts of flowers,
Sometimes I even think that she has super powers.

She likes champagne, sweet scents and roses,
She could be a model with all her poses.

She wears bright pink and frilly frocks,
She even has delicate pictures on her evening socks.

My mum likes those chocolates in the shape of a heart,
She always cuts them in half and gives me a part.

My mum, my mum, she's my role model,
The best thing she can give me is a long, warm cuddle.

Nicky Ghods (9)

My Dedication To You

M um - thank you so much for your ceaseless help and care
Y ou advice me, love me, you are always there

D rinks, food, you name it - it's provided for me by you
E veryone in our houses survives because of the jobs you do
D riving me everywhere - to clubs I attend
I t is always you who is generous, so much help you lend
C aring, forgiving, you have such a big heart
A lways ready for fun, I could not bear it if we did part
T rustworthy - that's you, I confide in you without fear
I nside or outside, you are always near
O nly you I tell my bad dreams and worries to
N obody knows how I feel - nobody but you

T errific and amazing, you always have something to give
O h, with you it is a pure pleasure to live

Y ear after year, a girl you've watched me become
O f all the people in the world, when I shout, you come
U nderstanding, dedicated - you are my loving mum!

Charlotte Malley (10)

My Cat Skimble

Skimble is my favourite cat,
She's soft and furry like a mat.
Her coat is orange, black and white
And she sleeps on my bed every night.

Her real name is Skimbleshanks
And she is always, always playing pranks.
She frowns when she's really cross,
Because she thinks that she's the boss.

She mostly attacks my tabby cat Molly,
To see this sight, is not very jolly.
She never walks, she'd rather run,
But oh, my cat is so much fun!

Her tail is like a squirrel's tail,
To catch a mouse, she'll never fail.
She comes home covered in leaves and twigs
And when I brush her, she dances three jigs.

I love my cat, as I'm sure you know,
The best time of year, is when she plays in the snow.
She really is my very best friend,
So this is where my poem ends.

Hannah Louise Timson (9)

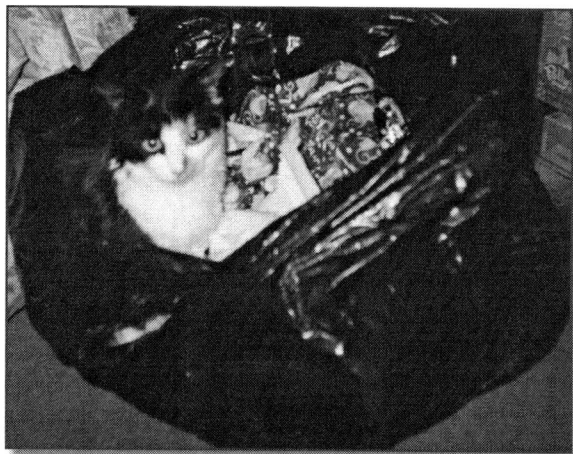

Poem For Dad

My dad is funny,
He thinks chips are yummy,
My dad's sound
And he likes a couple of pounds,
He is cool,
But sometimes a fool.

He likes Kiss who are a band,
But he's not tanned,
He can't swim in a pool,
But he's still really cool.
My dad's always in bed,
He's a lazy head,
My dad is married to my mum,
Who thinks cauliflower is yum, yum, yum!
He hates Liverpool,
That's why my dad's so cool!

Liam Jones (12)

Poem For Mum

It is very true,
That I would not be here,
If not for you,
This is for you Mum.

I remember every day,
As if it were just yesterday,
That you and I did many things,
This is for you Mum.

You are special to me,
Kind, loving and gracious,
You are cool,
This is for you Mum.

No matter what the age,
Or what the time,
You will be there,
This is you Mum.

Ruvarashe Samkange (14)

Mum

Mum you are the best,
Better than all the rest,
You are a super mum,
By always filling up my tum!

Always helping me when I'm stuck,
Even if I'm being a muck,
Working for me every day,
Even on holiday in May.

I've only got one more thing to say,
I love you, every day!

Lovelynn Ndlovu (8)

For Someone Special (My Stepdad)

I love my stepdad
He isn't that bad
Sometimes he is a pain
It makes me want to chase him down the lane
But I still love him.

Kirsty Winn (11)

Untitled

When I cut my knee,
Who was there to wipe it for me?
No one but my mother.

When I was in hospital,
Who was there to look after me?
No one but my mother.

When I was lonely,
Who was there to play with me?
No one but my mother.

Every day and every night
I have my mum to hug me tight.

Leonie Sparkes (8)

My Mum

When you need someone to listen,
When you need someone to care,
When you need someone to love you,
A mum is always there.

If you have done something wrong,
If you have done something bad
And don't know what to do,
A mum is always there.

When you need someone to talk to,
When you need someone to be there,
When you need someone to save you,
A mum is always there.

Diane King (12)

Woman

Oh! what a lovely mother you are,
You carried me in your womb for nine months,
You gave birth to me
And cared for me like an egg.

Oh! sweet mother,
My love for you is like water for the thirsty ones,
A day I don't see you,
I shed tears like a tree shedding her leaves.

Oh! my dear mother,
You are like the birds in the blue skies,
You are as beautiful as a rose,
You are as strict as a general.

Oh! my dear mother,
I will never forget you,
For you are as brave as a lion
And stronger than rocks.

Roland Bakoh Pivadga (14)

My Mum

My mum is sometimes happy
Sometimes even chatty

My mum is sometimes sad
And sometimes gets mad

My mum is sometimes funny
And makes me feel sunny

My mum is a light
That's really, really bright

My mum is the water
And I am her daughter

My mum is the rain
And sometimes is a pain

My mum is made of love
She is as pretty as a dove

My mum is the best
She is better than all the rest.

Nirvana Eden (10)

Dad

Dad, you're so special in every single way
Dad, you give me money when I go away
Dad, you're so cool
Dad, you love pool
Dad, you are so, so funny
Dad, you look like a bunny
Dad, you are the best
Dad, you're better than the rest.

Sian Hughes (12)

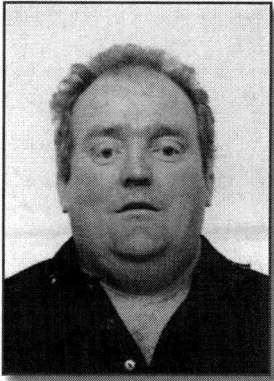

You're My Special Person

You are my special person,
I need you very much,
You're always there when I am down,
You have a special touch.

When I cry, you ask what's wrong
And hold me in your arms,
You make me laugh and cheer me up,
With your special charms.

We play together all the time
And have the best of fun,
The games we play, make us laugh,
You are my bestest chum!

We share our deepest secrets,
Just between us two,
No one knows except for us,
Our friendship must be true!

I'll always be there for you,
You'll always be there for me,
No one will come between us,
Forever we will be!

Victoria Mason & Jasmine Dixon (13)

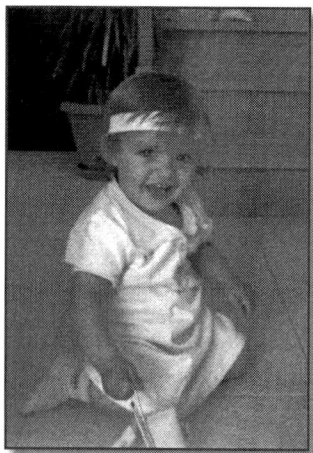

Someone Special

His special blue eyes
Make me fall into a daze,
I look at him sweetly
And sit back and gaze.

His skin is so soft,
His touch gives me chills,
I'm as proud as a queen,
On top of the hills.

His love is so precious,
It's like gleaming gold,
He was always there,
For me to hold.

We're like two of a kind,
Two peas in a pod,
Like everyone else,
He can be a right grumpy bod!

Once you've got him,
Don't let him go,
Believe in love
And let it show.

Now he's gone,
He's lying in his grave,
I love him so much,
He was ever so brave!

Kate Lancaster & Suzanne Davies (13)

Someone Special ... My Mum

M is for the million things she does for me
U is for the understanding, loving mother she is
M is also for making do with what she's got.

My mum is very special
I love her very much
She does such a lot for me
So now I'm giving something back.

Stephanie Brown (11)

Someone Special

Mum you're the best,
You're better than the rest,
I really want to show you,
How much I really love you,
I really think you're cool,
The other mums, they drool,
I really want to let you know,
I love you so.

She always forgets to do up her lace
And then she falls flat on her face,
She always tries to show off,
But all she does is blow off,
Then I look at her and think,
You really do stink!

Thomas Bayliss (11)

A Poem For You

There is a special day coming up . . .
A day dedicated to you,
When you can wind down, relax and chill,
Put your feet up,
Enjoy the mothering day.

I just want to say,
From all my extremities,
To my high and low points,
Your love is still the same.

Supporting, generous, loving you are,
Taking care of me,
Even ferrying me around,
Your love for us is consistent through the year.

On this mothering day,
You may not receive elegant gifts,
Or even the most expensive, materialistic items,
This does not mean I don't love you,
You'll be my mum each day of the year,
The years are more valuable than one day.

Amy Hadley (15)

Someone Special

Each star has a name,
You are called my mum,
I won't know how that feels,
Until my children call me mum.

Ellie Eveleigh (13)

Mum

Mum you are the greatest,
A shining, twinkly star,
You're totally cool,
You flippin' well rule!
You're the bestest mum by far.
If I need help with my homework
You are there to help me work.
I like watching you play the drums,
While I sit there eating plums.
You cook scrumptious spaghetti Bolognese,
It's really delicious with mayonnaise!
Badminton was your favourite sport
Only if everyone could see you in the court.
I don't know what I'd do without you;
You are my greatest, shimmering star!

Aisha Butt (9)

Someone Special

My mum always trusts me
Even if I burn down a tree
The long hours don't help much
When the car broke, she fixed the clutch
She works hard for a living
And still she's very giving
When my dad went, he left a letter
My grandad always said, she could do better!

Sebastian Moore

I Remember

Up and down, up and down
Dad swings me all around
And just before bed
A story is read

Up and down, up and down
Dad swings me all around
Scribbling in Nursery 2
That was the only drawing I could do

Up and down, up and down
Dad swings me all around
Dad and his friend are laying the lawn
Hacking through brambles and thorn

Up and down, up and down
Dad swings me all around
These memories in my head
Are kept even after they are said.

Zoë Seiffert (11)

Mr Right

I stared into his dreamy eyes
I hoped we would never say our goodbyes
He looked like a royal prince
I haven't even seen him since
He's the guy from my fortune cookie
He's as sweet as the sugar in my tea
He smiles when I wink at him
Did I say that his name is Jim?
His smile glistens in the light
As he holds me so tight
Every day I pray and pray
Till it comes to that special day
When we can picnic on the lawn
At the break of the dawn
He will wrap his arms around me
As we watch the sun set over the big blue sea.

Tierney Martin (11)

My Mum

My mum is the best person in the world
I can always go to her if I need anything
She has been there for me all my life
She takes me to school
Picks me up again.

Quite small
Red and black hair
Like my Tulketh tie!
Light brown eyes
Autumn leaves . . . like mine
Body piercing: exciting and fun
I love my mum.

She is very kind
Buys me everything
Looks after me all the time
Collette, thanks Mum!

Nathan Greenwood (13)

My Mum

My mum is really pretty
Really curly hair
Looks after me

I love her so much!
Her eyes are brilliant blue
Like the summer sky
Hair brown like autumn trees
She is sweet, like spring freesias.

Thanks Mandy!

Charmane Dean (14)

My Mum

My mum, she's great,
A lovely cook,
She bakes lots of cakes,
From the recipe book!

She helps me lots,
With friends and advice
And never gets mad,
When she has to repeat things twice!

My mum, I love her,
I'm glad she loves me too!
She always comforts me,
When I'm sad or blue.

And that is why,
I'd like to say . . .
A great big thank you
On Mother's Day!

Bronia Jane McGregor (11)

Mum, Mum

Mum, Mum,
You always seem to care,
Whenever I need you,
You are always there.

You always look out for me,
You make sure I'm OK,
You taught me how to be kind
And you taught me how to play.

Now you've taught me right from wrong,
It's time that you are told,
This poem has been dedicated,
To the best mum in the world.

Amber Roskilly (13)

My Mum

Thank you Mum for being there,
Whenever I'm in need.
Encouraging me when I am unsure,
Giving me the strength to succeed.

When life seems impossible
You wipe away my tears
And with gentle words of wisdom,
You soothe away my fears.

I'm sure I have said harsh words to you
When I've been angry and despairing,
But your love for me never falters,
You remain steadfastly kind and caring.

Thank you Mum for all the support
And the happy memories I treasure
I am so lucky to have your true love beyond measure!

Sian Riley-Phillips

This Person

Do you know this person who is all of this?
This person is so very kind.
Do you know this person?
This person is always there for me.
Do you know this person?
This person cares for me all of the time.
Do you know this person?
This person is so very good at cooking.
Do you know this person?
This person is ever so funny.
Do you know this person?
If you have not guessed who this person is . . .
It's my mum!

Liam Leavy (11)

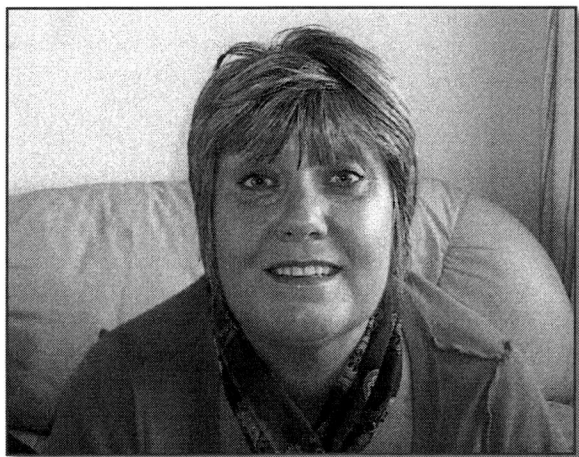

Flowers For My Mum

My mum is kind and thoughtful,
She's always there to help,
Looking after my brother and me,
Keeping a clean and tidy house.

She goes without, so we can have
The things we want so much,
I love my mum, I really do,
She deserves flowers by the bunch!

Katie West (11)

To My Mum

My magnificent mum,
My gorgeous mum,
My splendid mum,
My understanding mum,
My courageous mum,
My intelligent mum,
That's my mum!

James Walsh (9)

Mum

My mum is special, my mum is great
She's always there and never late
She's at my back, my guide, my light
She makes my world complete and bright.

Joe Roderick

My Mom

I love my mom, she is the best,
She takes me shopping to buy a new dress,
She looks after me and my family,
I love her and she loves me.

She cooks my food
And tidies my room,
Washes my clothes
And paints my toes.

When I am sad, she makes me glad,
We get in a huddle and have a great cuddle,
She gives me a kiss, whilst I make a wish.

We go on holiday together,
We make sandcastles whatever the weather,
We walk around the town at night,
Watching and shopping with delight.

Ellie Oldacre (11)

A Huge Thank You

Here's a poem to my one and only mum,
Saying a huge thank you for the great things she has done,
When she drops me off at school
And sees my great assemblies in the school,
When she gives me a new vest,
When she tells me to sit down and rest,
When she's waiting by the gates,
Talking to some of her mates,
Give a huge thank you to my mum!

Jodi Bungay (9)

Moyna

(Dedicated to my aunty)

Although she may not be my mum
she gives me advice
and shines on me like the rays of the shining sun!

Always giving me a shoulder to cry on
then passing a tissue
from the box beside her

My aunty is like my second mum
been there for me
since my journey in the world began

This person is so special to me
who lives in my heart as well as my life
she's just great
just like my mate

She's someone to really appreciate
together we laugh, joke
mess about, do our hair

bringing me up when I'm down
when I'm with her there's no reason to frown
thinking of this poem wasn't so hard
it's easy when the person is so simple to understand

I'm so lucky to have her
I guess it's just fate
so I'd gladly like to dedicate this poem
to Moyna my aunty that I love so much
thank you for being who you are
so don't ever change!

Tanjila Begum (13)

Mum

You're always, always there for me Mum,
When I'm sick or ill,
You really, really care for me Mum,
You're just like a happy pill.

You're really, really cool Mum,
You love to laugh and play,
You make me feel great Mum,
In every single way.

You never look bad or ugly Mum,
You're always on top of your game,
Even on your worst days,
You never make *me* insane.

Maybe one day when we're older,
I'll be able to pay you back,
'Cause I love you Mum and always will,
You're crazy, wild and wack!

Tom Williams (15)

Father's Hands

Father's hands, messy from work
Strong and gentle, big and soft.
Hands that hug me, hands that hold me
I feel so safe in my father's hands.

Father's hands, worn from holding
Drawing, designing, painting, making.
Hands that are tough and ready for anything
Always so brave, keeps it inside, for as long as he can.

Morgan Veazey (11)

My Sister

My sister is the best,
She's better than the rest.
My sister can be grumpy
And more than a little bit jumpy.
My sister's name is Jennifer
And I really, really like her.
We all call her Jenny
And for her birthday, she got way more than a penny!
She's nearly always at school,
Everyone knows she's not a fool
(And she's really good in the pool!)
She's 14, so that means she's a teenager,
I'm 10, so that means four years to be the age of her!
Jenny likes to dress in fashion
And for music, she has this *huge* passion.
She has long, strawberry-blonde hair,
Which will go with anything that she'll wear.
Jenny gets two weeks extra holiday,
In which she can go away,
(For that, I *sometimes* say, 'Hooray!')
And now for my last ending rhyme,
I will love her to the very end of time!

Lucy Cook (10)

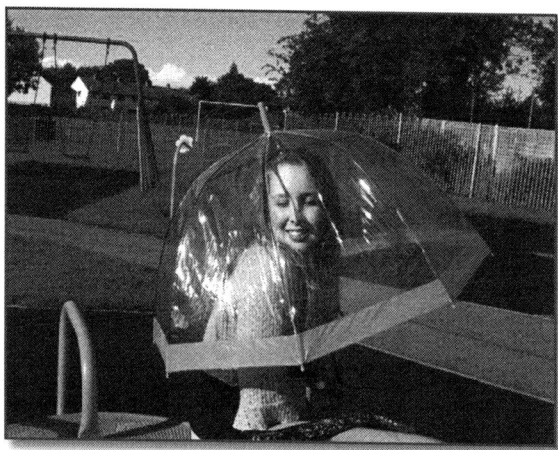

My Mum Is Unique!

My mum is like a flower,
Unique in every way.
She's always busy,
But not too busy for me.
Her heart is like a diamond,
Lighting up my path.
She is so cool
And funky too.
Her life is like a treacle sponge,
Slopping in every direction.
She inspires me to reach my goal in life.

My mum is all of these things,
But most of all, she is special and I belong to her.

Zoe Hyde (10)

Someone Special

Someone special would be my mum
She cheers me up if I am glum
She helps me if I need help
And always comforts me from things that are frightening
And things that are sad
But is always supportive if I am glad
Glad about something that I have done
Like the first time I ever won my first run
That was a very exciting time
Having everyone congratulate me on what I had done
So please, please understand
That mums are the greatest
Someone for me and everyone.

Lucy Pratt (12)

A Poem About My Mum

My mum wears perfumes from Hajj which smells like a rose,
She prays five times a day like a praying machine,
She hates sports for the reason that she isn't a sports fan,
My mum wears a scarf so as not to show her hair to men
when she goes out,
She likes to go to Bangladesh on a vacation to visit
her ancient parents,
And have a break from doing most of the chores,
My mum doesn't have a job, but she looks after us
And we look after her as a senior lady.

Mohammed Ali Ahmed (11)

Poem For Mum!

Mum, you are kind and caring,
Funny and helpful,
Always there for me,
You work so hard,
Doing voluntary work,
From the goodness of your heart.
I wish one day, I'll be like you,
Doing nursing and first aid.
When I say, 'I hate you!'
I love you a great deal.
When I'm feeling sad,
I just want you, *Mum!*

Amy Louise Livingstone-Lawn (12)

My Mum

My mum is so much fun,
She does a lot for me,
My mum shines like the sun,
She fills me up with glee.

She tries to make up some jokes,
But they aren't really funny,
When I'm good, she takes me out
And I spend all her money.

She loves chocolate,
She has some all the time,
When I don't do as I'm told,
She always has a whine.

Even though she can be a pest,
My mum, she is still the best!

Maddie Flinn (10)

What Mums Are Really Like

Mums are always there for you,
They're loving, caring and sweet to you,
When you're sad, you have a mum to go to
And when your mum's sad, you go to them too,
You can't live without a mum because they're always beside you,
So mums are the number ones in the world
And mums do everything for you.

Aneela Aziz (13)

My Mum

My mum is the best
She can be a pest
But I still love her
My mum brings me things
But she always sings.

My mum always prays
She says the right thing
I love my mum
I look up to my mum
Also she knows her sums
My mum is the best.

Zara Mahmood (11)

The World's Greatest Mum!

Why my mum is great . . .
We spend time with each other
Me and Mum are just like best mates,
I would be lost without her

She will be there for me,
She helps me with my homework,
Especially when it comes to do RE,
She cleans the house so it's nice and clean

I would be lost without her,
I don't know what I'd do,
If anyone mistakes her for Sir,
I will get so angry, red and I'll roar

I like helping when she's cleaning, seeing that it's clean,
I like to help my mum,
She's like a lean, clean, spinning machine,
That's why everything's perfect

I also have a brother, but I'm the mummy's girl,
We spend time together, nearly 24/7,
We like watching telly, especially 'The Bill',
We like it when we take trips out, girlie trips that rule

No one can split up us,
Not even my brother,
I always make her a cup of tea, in her favourite cup,
She rules!

Monica Rai (11)

Untitled

My mum is fab
Even though she is mad
And she is glad
No one is a peach like my mum
My mum can bake
She is like a chef
She bakes cakes with me
I like my mum
She is beautiful
And joyful and cheerful
I like my mum
She is great!

Katie Emma Deeble (7)

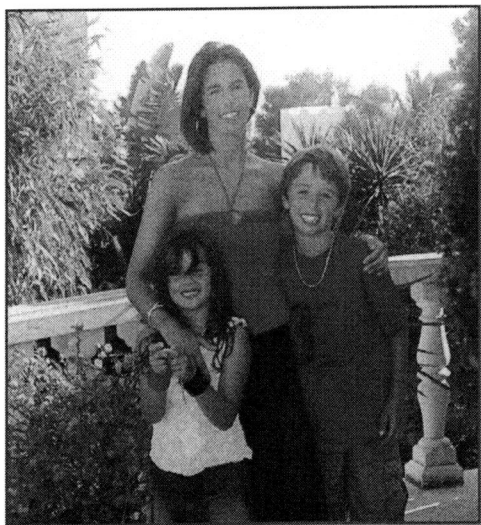

This Is For My Mum

This is to my mum
Who lets me sit in the sun
And lets me eat a sticky bun
Which is yum, yum, yum
She even lets me chew gum
Which is also yum, yum, yum
She is very, very, very, very fun!

Mum's going to have a baby soon
She said she's going to have it on the moon
She said she's going to get a balloon
In the afternoon and have it on the moon!
She is the best!

Maddie Bethany Blake (9)

Someone Special

My someone special is my mum,
She's happy and glad like the sun,
I love her because she is my mum,
She helps me when I am sad or glum,
I love her because she is my mum,
Therefore, she *is* my special one!

Ashton Dawes (12)

Naughty Or Nice

Half of the time I am an angel
Half of the time I am a devil
Sometimes I am really nice
Sometimes I am really naughty

I could be helping others
Or even playing practical jokes
Some people like me
Some people don't

There is always one person
Who loves me either way
And even when I don't know it
That person is my mum.

Louise Smith (17)

Just For You Mum

Mum you're special to me in so many ways,
There's times you've made me cry,
But you still give me so much joy,
You're always there for me,
Forever that will be,
You brought me up into this world,
With everything I need, especially love,
You cook and clean
And I appreciate that very much,
You may scream and shout,
But I can understand all of that,
There are loads of lovely words that can describe you,
You're wonderful, beautiful and kind-hearted,
I'm so glad that you're my mum,
You may not be perfect,
But to me you're as perfect as can be,
This poem is from me to you, from the bottom of my heart,
I've always tried to say how thankful I am
For everything that you do for me,
So thank you very much,
As I am at the end of my poem,
I was writing it to you,
Just to tell you how much I really love you.

Jade Shallow (14)

A Poem For My Mum

M y mum is a fabulous sailor
Y ummy cakes she makes

M um is always there to help me
U nderstands any problems
M y marvellous, magnificent mum!

Georgina Tall (10)

My Mother

My mom is the best of all,
She'll care and love me and will comfort me when I fall,
Our love is too much to say,
But hopefully, she will know that every day,
In bad and good times, I will always be a part of you,
I love and care for you, whatever you say or do,
When we get on each other's nerves,
We will still love each other as much as at first,
Your eyes remind me of the calm countryside,
That one day, we'll get to see,
But of course, being in your arms is better than all to be,
Your heart reminds me of me, because once I was inside you
And forever I will long to be.

Sabrina Pisuto (11)

I'd Do Anything For Mum!

I'd do anything for my mum,
She's the best mum ever!

She cooks, she cleans,
She makes the place sparkle and gleam.

She cares and she helps,
She's the best mum ever!

Emma Loughran (8)

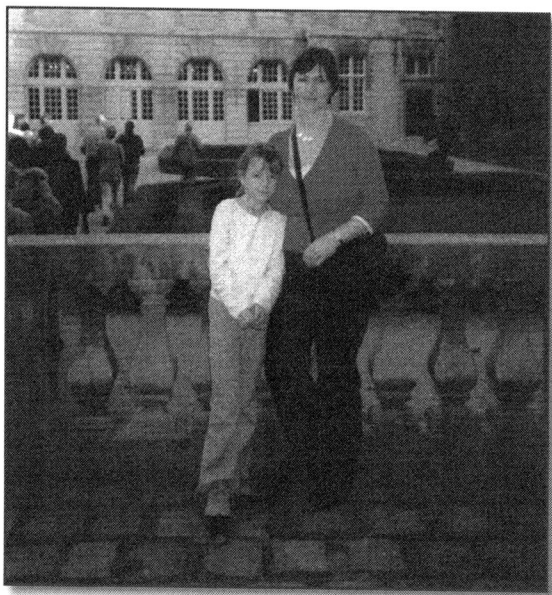

For My Friend

Friendship is much more than brains
It's much more than cars
It's much more than money can buy
It's generously found in the heart

In the heart of a friend
Is the heart of the other
Where two worlds collide
To form an enormous universe

It's not less than health
Not less than jewellery or ice
It shines like the sun
And sparkles like the stars

You, my friend, are all I have
And all I rely upon
With you, my friend, I am who I am
'Cause only you can complete me.

Keji Ogunrinde (15)

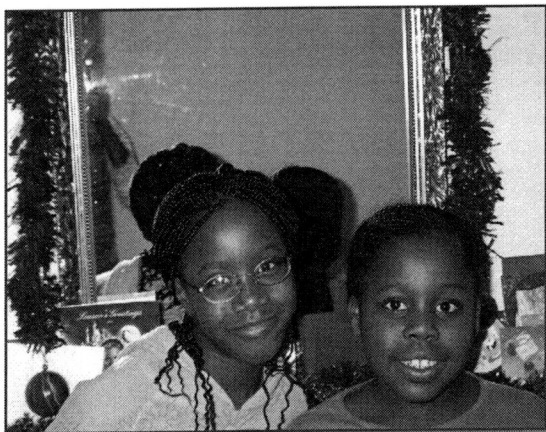

My Dad

My dad is very special,
He is working all the time,
On his day off, he takes us fishing
And helps us with our line.

He puts food on the table
And puts coal on the fire,
He takes me to concerts,
With the school choir.

Dad is the best
And helps me all the time,
I like him so much
And that is why I am writing this rhyme.

Michaela Protheroe (12)

Heather

H is for happy and healthy all the time
E is for enjoyment as you play with me
A is for always a friend
T is for tears that we cried when we were split apart
H is for horses at the stables and when we play it outside
E is for every moment together
R is for a real best friend.

Bethany Chuter (10)

My Dad Is ...

My dad is,
Not interested in bling,
My dad is,
Never hurt by a sting.

My dad is,
Always driving his bus,
My dad is,
Never in a fuss.

My dad is,
Always loaded with money,
My dad is,
Very, very funny,
My dad is,
Never in a hurry.

Katy-Leigh Bogin (11)

Well Done Dad

Well done Dad,
You embarrass me when things are bad.

Well done Dad,
You drive us all mad.

Telling daft jokes and being rude again
And sometimes you drive us totally insane.

Well done Dad,
For being there for me
And making me see.

When life wasn't worth it,
You went out and hurt it.

Well done Dad,
Now I see,
All these things you did for me.

Well done Dad,
You remind me of all the things I don't want to know,
But we all really know.

Well done Dad,
You're not all that bad,
Well done Dad!

Laura Dean (15)

A Great Mum

I'm sure your mum's great,
But mine's even better,
She'll come out and play with us,
In any kind of weather.

And when we have snow,
What fun we have,
After playing in it all afternoon,
We get hot chocolate and a nice, warm bath.

The cakes she makes are such a treat,
Ones that no other mum can ever beat,
I'm so glad that she's my mum,
'Cause she is my very best chum.

Hannah Bardsley (9)

Mum

I would give as a gift:
The first snowdrop in spring,
A shady tree in the heat of the sun,
The last autumn leaf to fall
And a unique snowflake in winter.

I would give as a gift:
The last breath of a loved one,
The first cry of a newborn baby,
The first steps of a toddler,
The excitement on Christmas Eve.

I would give as a gift:
The smell of home-made biscuits,
The warmth of the fire,
The fresh dew on the grass
And the bitter taste of a lemon.

I would wrap my gift in:
A woolly blanket,
Because it's warm and soft,
It will keep my gift,
Safe and comfortable.

My gift would be:
Carried through the clouds,
Passing through starlit skies,
By an angel,
Who will gently lay it by my mum's side.

A priceless gift,
For a priceless mum.

Sarah Loughran (12)

My Mum

My mum is kind
My mum is sweet
My mum keeps me on my feet
She loves me, cares for me
But she always gives me love
What more could you want!

Indiana MacKenzie (10)

Dad

He's a person with a great taste in wine,
He's a master with the cooking,
He's a helping hand all the time,
He's there if you fancy a laugh,
He's there if you want to go out,
He knows where the best chip shop is,
He knows where the best beaches are,
He knows where to go for a walk,
He knows what to do in general,
Sure, he's daft, sure, he's silly
And
He is always there!

James Peacock (11)

Love You Gran!

L ast time I saw you, you gave me a cake
O nly loved it because it reminded me of you
V aluable as you may be, you're
E verything a grandchild will need

Y esterday I saw you, you brought tears to my eyes
O nly you can say hello and make me smile
U nderstandably you are the greatest

G ran you are so important
R ainy days you keep me safe
A mazing sweets you give me
N othing can get between us, because you're my gran.

Maryam Shahban (10)

Long Live Gran!

There was a plague, where people slaved and animals died,
My grandma lived to see the day,
When famine and draught cursed the world,
A tragedy struck, as close family and friends passed away,
One of her six pearled daughters also did not live to see another day,
But Gran still survived until 1976,
When she moved to England
And improved a new life,
Until one day, she had a granddaughter (me),
Then she loved and cherished me,
Like her own long-lost . . . daughter!

Anisa Shahban (13)

My Perfect Dad!

Thank you for being there
When I need you,
You care for me and comfort me
In every single way.
When I'm sick
You are always there to make me feel better,
I am the luckiest person in the world
Because you are my dad!

Sophie Dunne (10)

Moggy

(Dedicated to Adam Morris, whose life was taken at the young age of 19, whilst on active duty in Iraq)

You were a good friend
A true hero to all
A soldier who served
His Queen and country
Even though you died so young
Your memory will live on
In the hearts and souls
Of the nation

The British Army
Will be proud of you
And your fellow men
Who have died in the fight
For what is right

The thoughts of friends and relatives
Will live on with the memories of you.

Natasha Hickson (17)

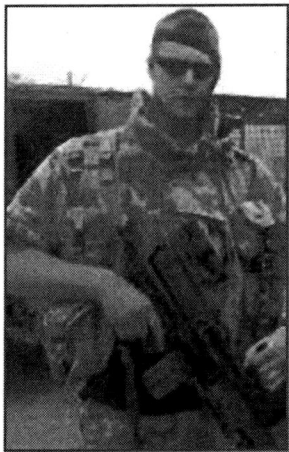

My Dad

My dad is really funny,
My dad is a really good cook,
My dad is really good at maths,
My dad is a busy man,
My dad, I love my dad.

Lauren Butler (9)

Yo Ross!

My man Ross here's a poem for you,
When I'm with you, I'm never blue,
Check it out, you're loads of fun,
Man, you make me feel as bright as the sun.

Ross, Ross,
Yeeeaaahhh!
Ross, Ross,
Yeah!

Sometimes we go racing down the Lane,
Even though the skateboard I ride is a pain,
Your go-kart's cool, it really is,
When you ride it, you go whiz!

Ross, Ross,
Yeeeaaahhh!
Ross, Ross,
Yeah!

Connor Parsons (10)

Day By Day

Day by day she glittered in the sun
Day by day I saw her have lots of fun
Day by day she shined with passion
Day by day she had good fashion

Day by day her hair waved in the wind
Day by day she showed her bling
Day by day he looked upon her
Day by day he never went wrong by her.

Samuel Morgan (9)

The Coolest Mum

The coolest mum is my mum
The greatest mum is my mum
Cos when I need her any day
She is always by my side

When I am ill I get treated dearly
She is pretty if it's not the morning
I am taken to places I love to visit
And bought things that are needed and wanted

She is kind and loving at all times
And wanted every day
Gives me sweets when I fancy them
And says yes and not may

My mum sounds lovely
My mum sounds kind
My mum sounds funky
And she really doesn't mind

I think my mum rocks
And is always there to stick with me too
And to love me at all times
So Mum, I think we should hang out, just me and you!

Kirsty Balaam (11)

Mums Are The Best

My mum is great, I have to say,
She's there to talk and to play,
I'd like to start by describing my mum,
She's pretty, funny and never very glum.

She's the best at rounders and gets lots of runs
And then she hands out very sticky buns!
Her happiness and loveliness will never, ever end,
She really is my best, best friend!

I love my mum, she's special to me,
The best mum there could ever be!

Charlie Dale (10)

My Mum

Mums are special,
Mums are great,
But you're the one,
I appreciate.

So as a little thank you,
I would really like to say:
'You're my lovely mummy,
Who I love lots every day!'

Rebecca Simmons (10)

My Mum

My mum is caring
My mum is loving
She buys me berries
And takes me to Uncle Larry

My mum is fantastic
We both watch films about Atlantic
My mum buys me chocolate when we go shopping
She takes me to Pizza Hut
And buys me a pizza with extra topping!

My mum is cool
She is not a fool
My mum is bright
And makes things right

My mum is perfect
She's always worth it
My mum is nice
She gives me advice

Thank you, Mum!

Ogaga Blessing Otuorimuo (9)

My Mother

My mother has a big head
At least she makes my bed
She is as cold as snow
She has a friend called Moe
She reads a lot of books
She says, 'Stay away from the hooks'
My mother shouts and I go in a pout
I go down the shop
And my mother buys a bottle of pop
I used to have a buggy
Now my mother takes me to rugby
She does not lie to me
Half the time she needs a wee
She buys me books all the time
Especially the ones that rhyme
She takes me to school every day
Because I have dinners, she has to pay
I love you Mum, I really do
I am glad my wish has come true.

Alexandra Jade Samuel (9)

Mother

M y mother is as sweet as my girlfriend
O ther mothers cannot be better than mine
T ogether we are a team
H appy as can be
E yes likes stars
R ushes to town to beat the crowds.

Liam Roberts (9)

Mother

My mother is as happy as ham
By the way, she hates lamb
My mother is as sweet as sugar
Not just that, she is full of laughter
My mother is as cool as a cat
And she hates to wear a floppy hat
My mother is as playful as pancakes
And she just loves the landscapes
My mother is as dull as a doughnut
But she is as sweet as a coconut
My mother is as cute as candyfloss
And kills all the moths
My mother is as pleasant as peas
I've got to say she's prettier than me
My mother is as lively as a lollipop
But I've got to say she wears lovely tops
My mother is as lovely as a lily
And loves to be silly
My mother is as helpful as honey
And is so funny
I love you, Mum, cos you're the best ever!

Sacha Horn (9)

Mother

She's gentle and pretty
She's the best in the West
When I am ill
She treats me well
She loves me a lot and if I were to die
Her heart would break
She plays with me
She takes me out
She makes me safe all the time
She sings songs and loves to dance
She gives me delicious, tasty food
My mum's the best
In the whole wide world
That's my mum
She's the best thing I ever had
The way she is
Is the way I want her to be.

Sam Durke (9)

A Little Girl Needs A Daddy

A little girl needs a daddy,
For many, many things;
Like holding her high off the ground,
Where the sunlight sings!

Like being the deep music,
That tells her all is right;
When she awakens frantic
With the terrors of the night!

Like being the great mountain,
That rises in her heart;
And shows her how she might get home,
When all else falls apart.

Like giving her the love,
That is hers;
So diving deep or soaring high,
She'll always find him there
And always and everywhere!

Simpal Korana (16)

Poem About My Dad

My dad is as quick as lightning
He can be very frightening

He is as clever as a rocket scientist
But not dumb enough to be electrocuted

He is as nice as a soft, cuddly bear
But not too rough to give you messy hair

His mind is so kind, if you get lost
His love would be able to find you

He holds you so warm, it will never be cold
He loves me more than the whole wide world.

Eliot Gannon (12)

Poem For My Dad

Dad, this is just a poem to say thank you for the past years,
How helpful you were when you and mum split up,
You always did something to make me cheer up.

When I was bored with nothing to do,
You would always make something out of nothing for *us* to do,
When we go out on a fishing trip,
We mostly have good luck,
But for the past few weeks we've had bad.

I love spending time with you,
With whatever we have to do,
I love you Dad and just again,
Thank you!

Jake Michel (12)

My Dad The Great

My dad the great,
My very best mate,
I think of him always,
When I walk through his hallways,
I know he loves me,
Because we were meant to be,
But sometimes, I just wish he was here with me.

Craig Corbally (12)

My Dad

My dad is cool,
My dad is the best,
But sometimes he's angry
And he gets in a mess.

He taught me how to ride a bike
And to skate,
He hates chocolate bars
And he has a nice company car.

Alec le Vannais (13)

Dad!

I like you Dad, you can be funny
You make my blue days turn to sunny
I know you shout, but without a doubt
You're still a really good Dad.

Dad you're great
You help me a lot
With homework, with quizzes
With anything really!

So, thank you Dad
For being so kind
For being so helpful
Thank you Dad!

Enya Ferey (12)

Mothers

My mummy is sweet,
Clever and kind
And sometimes
Completely off her mind!

She is the warmth in a smile
And the twinkle in black skies,
I know she loves me,
I can see it in her eyes.

She is sweet like candy
And yummy like cheese,
She always says thank you
And she always says please.

She takes me out,
Because we like the sun,
She chases me around,
Because she's lots of fun.

I had fun when I was young,
With me, Dad and Mummy,
Till my mad sister,
Came in Mummy's tummy!

Emily Elaine Phillips (9)

Mother's Day

M y mother is kind and gentle
O h she loves flowers
T idies my bedroom for me
H appy Mother's Day
E ats my leftovers
R ubbish she puts in the bin
S ausage and mash she makes me

D ogs are a pain my mother says
A lways helping me on my homework
Y et she has been kind to me this year.

Noel Warlow (9)

For My Dad

You have always been there for me,
To help me with lots of things,
You take me out to places,
Wherever I want to go,
You take me swimming,
You take me dipping,
You get me chocolate all the time,
You are my only dad
And will always be there for me.

Ryan Pijiura (13)

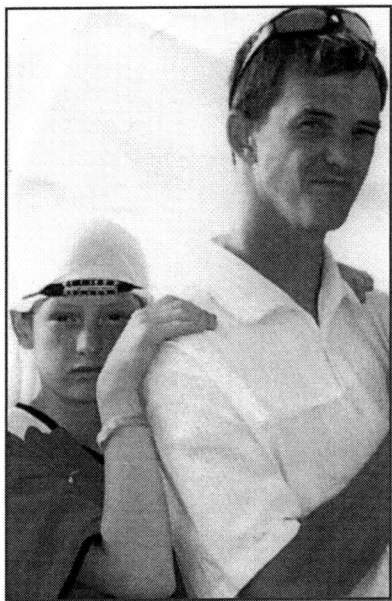

Someone Special

Dad I'm lucky,
Dad I'm glad,
To have someone like you,
As my dad.

You're the one who cares for me,
You're the one who loves me,
Dad you really are someone special.

You're the one who makes me smile,
You're the one who understands me,
You're the one I can trust,
Dad you really are someone special.

Any man can be a father,
But it takes a real man,
Someone special, to be a dad,
You are special and I love you!

Niamh Hocking (12)

For My Dad

You are the best,
Above *all* the rest,
You are not crazy
And of course, not lazy,
You take me swimming,
Just to go and dip in,
You get Galaxies all the time
And you sometimes smell like slime,
But you are my only dad
And always will be . . .

Kyle Bourne (12)

Dad

Dad you're great
Dad you're helpful
Without you I would not be here
I love you loads every single day
I will always be here for you no matter what
I hope you love me like I love you
No matter what happens through our life
I hope you'll always be there for me when I need you
I will never forget what you told me when you moaned at me
When we were having fun and laughing our heads off
It will always be in my memories.

Andreia de Barros (13)

My Dad

My dad is the best,
Better than all the rest,
The memories we have are fun,
Like when we used to go on the run,
I hope I see you soon.

You're someone who cares,
You've always been there for me,
You taught me to ride my bike
And you used to take me to the park,
I hope I see you soon.

Paige Smith (13)

My Dad

I miss him when I'm away,
I really want to stay,
With him I feel safe,
I know he has faith in me.

Football mad,
That's my dad,
Running around,
On the football ground.

I love him lots,
He loves me too,
I'll always love him,
Through and through!

Amy Le Moignan (12)

My Dad

My dad is amazing,
He gives up anything for me,
When I ask for help, he helps me,
He is the coolest by far,
He drives a trendy car.

He's always there for me when I'm upset,
I feel safe when I'm with him,
He loves me for who I am
Not what other people want me to be.

Helping me when I am sad
I am happy that he is there
Football mad, my dad, he is so funny
When they score a goal
I love my dad so much.

Demi Bolton (11)

Dad

You are my taxi,
You take me everywhere,
You taught me how to swim
And you care for me.

You put food on my plate,
Which I ate,
You've cared for me all these years
And you really care.

Connor Dunne (12)

My Dad

The thing I like about my dad,
He never really gets mad.
He's too busy being funny
And spending all his money,
I really love my dad!

Dads are wonderful people you know
When you're a kid, you don't wanna let go,
Playing games outside,
Or hide-and-seek inside,
Thank you Dad!

Dads love to entertain,
That I can't explain,
But one thing he loves to do,
Is to argue,
But he is my dad!

My dad is a loving, caring man,
Bringing me up as best he can,
I love you for this,
The fun I wouldn't miss,
You're a wonderful dad!

Emily Michel (12)

My Dad!

My dad is very clever,
My dad is very funny,
That is what he's like -
My wonderful dad!

He helps with my homework,
He tells some funny jokes,
That is what he's like -
My wonderful dad!

I say thank you to you
And I love you too!

Sharon Howarth (13)

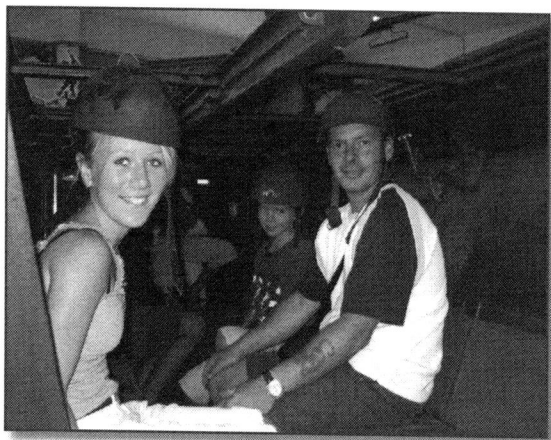

My Poem About My Dad!

My dad is funny,
He used to call me honey,
He always makes me laugh
And he doesn't like a bath,
He only likes the shower
And he is in there for half an hour,
He's never smelly,
But he has a little beer belly,
Thank you, Dad, for being so mad
Giving me lifts to town
And not making me sad,
Thank you, for making me laugh
And making me, in winter, wear a scarf,
Thank you, for being funny
And making me a happy bunny!

Jody Brown (12)

My Dad

My dad ain't the coolest
But one thing he does
He looks after me for everything
And he has a real buzz

Thank you for picking me up
In the cold and rain
And for looking after me
When I'm in great pain.

Timothy Houiellebecq (13)

My Dad

My dad isn't a superhero
He's just an average guy
But without him
My world wouldn't go by.

I love my dad very much
And he loves me too
What do you think?
Would you like to meet him too?

Jake Le Caudey (13)

Mother

My mother is sweet, the only one I want to kiss
My mother is as cute as candy and as sweet as me
My mother is as sweet as a crunchy cherry
My mother is cuter than me and you
My mum is as cool as a funny monkey
My mum is as sweet as a lump of sugar
My mum is the best
My mum is as cool as cold, cold ice
My mum is cooler than cats
My mum irons my clean shirts
My mum bathes me.

Demi-Jade Murnieks (8)

A Poem About My Mom

My mom is the best
She makes me laugh and giggle
She is a diamond in my heart
And stays with me in the middle.

Danika Wheatley (11)

My Number One Mum

My mum is so good to me
I love her more than ever
I will keep her forever
She's always there for me
Whenever I need her
I don't know what I would do if I lost her
She's the best, even though she can be a pest
She's very good
I wouldn't be able to find another
She sorts my problems out for me
She's brought me up since I was born
And now I'm 12
All these years she's made promises
And has never let me down
I'm glad I've got such a caring mum
She's stood by my side to keep me safe and sound
I love you, my number one mum
Thanks for being my number one mum!

Abigail Bywater (12)

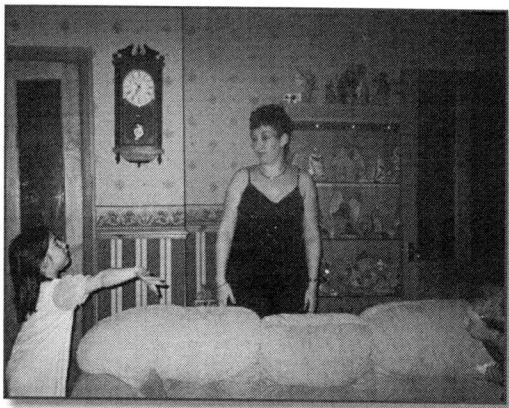

The Person I Admire . . .

The person I admire is my mum,
She cheers me up when I'm feeling glum.
She's got this warm glow,
But she's not got any foe.
No matter how busy she'll be,
She always listens to me.
She can't stand a frown,
She'll never let you down.
She's just perfect all the way round!

Nazia Begum (11)

Mom I Love You

Mom I love you,
Not only in cooking and cleaning,
But in everything you do.

Mom you're the best,
But maybe lie down
And get some rest.

Mom I'm grateful for everything you give,
That's why I love you,
We're together to live.

Ellie Murphy (10)

Mum

I love my mum,
I came from her tum.
She simply is the best,
She is better than the rest.
I do not mean to brag,
But it is her to whom I nag!

She simply is divine,
But me, I'm just a swine.
I would not know what to do,
If Mum, I ever did lose you,
You keep me safe, no matter where we are,
Even if that be one thousand miles afar.

So Mum, oh Mum, please hear me out,
I know how much I scream and shout.
But Mum, oh Mum, I love you,
You're always there for me.
That's why I know no matter what happens,
Mum, oh Mum, *I will always love you!*

Charlene Readman (13)

Young Writers Information

We hope you have enjoyed reading this book - and that you will continue to enjoy it in the coming years.
If you like reading and writing poetry and short stories drop us a line, or give us a call, and we'll send you a free information pack. Alternatively, if you would like to order further copies of this book or any of our other titles, then please give us a call or log onto our website at **www.youngwriters.co.uk**

Young Writers, Remus House, Coltsfoot Drive, Woodston,
Peterborough PE2 9JX
Tel (01733) 890066

Email youngwriters@forwardpress.co.uk